Francisco Pizarro

and the Conquest of the Inca

Explorers of New Worlds

Francisco Pizarro
and the Conquest of the Inca

Gina DeAngelis

Chelsea House Publishers
Philadelphia

Prepared for Chelsea House Publishers by:
OTTN Publishing, Stockton, N.J.

CHELSEA HOUSE PUBLISHERS
Production Manager: Pamela Loos
Art Director: Sara Davis
Director of Photography: Judy L. Hasday
Managing Editor: James D. Gallagher
Senior Production Editor: J. Christopher Higgins
Series Designer: Keith Trego
Cover Design: Forman Group

3 5 7 9 8 6 4 2

Library of Congress Cataloging-in-Publication Data

DeAngelis, Gina
   Francisco Pizarro and the conquest of the Inca / Gina
   DeAngelis
      p.   cm. – (Explorers of new worlds)
Includes bibliographical references and index.
ISBN 0-7910-5951-0 (hc) – ISBN 0-7910-6161-2 (pbk.)
1. Pizzaro, Francisco, ca. 1475-1541–Juvenile literature.
2. Peru–History–Conquest, 1522-1548–Juvenile literature. 3. Incas–Juvenile literature. 4. Governors–Peru–
Biography–Juvenile literature. 5. Explorers–Peru–Biography–Juvenile Literature. 6. Explorers–Spain–Biography–Juvenile literature. [1. Pizzaro, Francisco, ca. 1475-
1541. 2. Explorers. 3. Peru–History–Conquest, 1522-
1548. 4. Incas. 5. Indians of South America.] I. Title.
II. Series.

F3442.Ptt6 D43 2000
985'.02'092–dc21
[B]   00-043076

Contents

Empire of
the Sun God

As the Spanish soldiers with Francisco Pizarro journeyed through the Inca empire, located in modern-day Peru, they saw many sights, such as this lake high in the Andes Mountains.

I

In the early 1500s, the brilliant city of Cajamarca stood in the middle of what is now Peru. When a small party of Spaniards made their way to Cajamarca in 1531, the wealth of the Inca people who lived there was clearly visible. These Spaniards were the first Europeans to see the city of Cajamarca, and they were stunned by its splendor, cleanliness, and organization. Inca buildings glimmered in the sun, and thatched-roof houses made from stone or **adobe** lined straight streets. Attractive stone temples and plazas paid homage to the sun god Inti. Tens of thousands of people lived in Cajamarca. The Spanish soldiers could tell that the city was heavily **populated** because they saw thousands of buildings.

Francisco Pizarro, the leader of the Spaniards, was a shrewd and ambitious man who was eager for adventure and glory. For years, Spanish explorers of Central America and the Caribbean had heard tales of wealthy natives living in lands to the south. Pizarro and his men had seen native stores of gold themselves years before, in 1524, when they landed at Tumbes, a city on the northwest coast of South America. Now, in 1531, the thought of riches drowned out whatever fears Pizarro and his fellow explorers may have had about continuing their journey into the heart of the Inca empire.

The Inca civilization was not the first to inhabit this region. Other peoples had settled in the rough climates of western South America at least 12,000 years before the Inca. A succession of cultures, such as the Chavín, Tihuanaco, Paracas, Nazca, Moche (or Mochica), and Chimú, flourished along the coastline and in the highlands of the Andes Mountains. The Inca civilization was built on the achievements of these earlier cultures.

According to Inca legend, in about A.D. 1200, Manco Capac, the son of the sun god, brought his people out of mountain caves and down into the valley. There he founded a new settlement in what later became the city of Cuzco. Each successive leader of the people who settled in this area was believed to be a *descendant* of Manco Capac, and he was called the Inca, which means "chief." The name was later used to describe the chief's followers, and the leader became known as the "Sapa Inca."

By about 1400, the Inca had barely expanded from Cuzco by conquering a few neighboring groups. But their civilization grew more complex over that time. Many different trades and specialized professions developed, and crafts such as pottery, fabric-making, and metalwork thrived.

The Sapa Inca was a godlike figure, and he ruled with absolute power. Inca society was highly regimented. For example, all Inca men were required to work for five years for the Sapa Inca; this period was known as a *mita*. No one was allowed to be lazy; even children and the elderly had work to do. But the Sapa Inca was a *benevolent* ruler. Despite the restrictions on individual freedoms, he provided food, clothing, and housing for everyone under his rule. No one starved or was homeless. The aged, sick, and widowed were provided for, as were Inca priests and government workers.

As time went by, the Inca empire grew by absorbing other peoples. During the 1400s, Inca civilization expanded rapidly under the warrior chief Yupanqui. After subduing a military threat from the Chanca people who lived north of the Inca, Yupanqui was named emperor Pachacuti (which means "World Reverser"). Pachacuti established an official Inca language, called *Quechua*, and he began a long period of expansion that lasted for a century. His son, Topa Inca, expanded the empire even farther, to the west and to the south, reaching deep into present-day Chile. In

> **When the Inca defeated neighboring tribes, they mostly left them alone. Conquered tribes had to follow Inca laws, pay taxes to the Inca government, and worship the sun as the Inca did. Otherwise, they were allowed to maintain their own cultures. Often, the living standards of the other groups were improved, because Inca culture was more advanced than their own.**

The Inca warrior-chief Yupanqui helped to expand the borders of the empire throughout Peru in the 15th century. He is also called Pachacuti, which means "World Reverser."

the early 1500s Topa Inca's son, Huayna Capac, expanded into present-day Ecuador, to the north.

By that time the Inca empire stretched over 2,500 miles along the western coast of South America, through jungles and mountains, from coastal deserts to inland rivers. The Inca named their empire Tahuantinsuyu, meaning "Land of the Four Quarters." More than 10 million people lived within the empire's borders, but most were descendants of conquered peoples. One historian estimates that only about 40,000 were of true Inca descent.

To control such a vast area, information and messages had to travel to and from the emperor quickly. The Inca built a remarkable system of roads that included many things we think of as modern: suspension bridges, roadside "rest stops," and road-side markers. The Inca did not have horses and did not know about the wheel, so to move or carry things they relied on manpower. Runners slept in huts placed at intervals along the roads so that they could be ready to carry any important message or object, day or night, wherever it needed to go.

The Inca were one of the most advanced civilizations in North or South America. In addition to specialized occupations, arts and crafts, and a system of roads, they also created ***relief maps*** made out of clay, carefully devised a calendar based on the sun's movement, and built canals and tunnels for

The Inca were skilled craftspeople. Their artisans created many beautiful objects, such as this gold toucan statuette.

irrigation. They used fertilizer to grow crops such as potatoes, yams, peanuts, and corn. They made fabric from cotton plants and from the wool of *alpacas* and llamas, using dyes to color it and embroidery to decorate it. They mined and *smelted* gold and silver, working the metals into beautiful objects and ornaments. The nobles among the Inca wore finely worked gold jewelry and headdresses containing beautiful feathers taken from rare birds.

Census-takers, called *quipu-camayoc*, recorded the numbers of people, animals, land holdings, and other resources in the Inca empire on a system of knotted strings, called *quipu*. The Inca army was well organized and experienced. Men from the other cultures living under the Inca joined the well-trained Inca army, and their people served the Sapa Inca in exchange for protection from invasion.

Pizarro arrived in the region during a time of great division among the Inca people. An earlier group of Spanish explorers had brought a deadly European disease (probably smallpox) to South America. The disease spread among the Inca, who had never been exposed to it and therefore had not developed *immunity*. It killed thousands of them, including their leader, Huayna Capac. Huayna's sons, Atahualpa and Huáscar, fought a bloody *civil war* over which of them would assume the title of Sapa Inca. When Pizarro and his crew arrived in 1532, Atahualpa had just defeated and imprisoned his brother.

Atahualpa had heard about the arrival of white men almost as soon as they landed. Using the Inca system of runners, messengers reached the Sapa Inca within a day. The runners reported all the doings of the strange, white-skinned men. The strangers were said to be arriving on land in large floating houses with wings (these were actually their sailing ships). And they wore metal clothing (armor) and carried sticks that produced both thunder and flashes like lightning (guns). But the Inca were most shocked when they saw the Spaniards riding on horseback. The natives had never seen horses before. To them the Spanish soldiers on horseback seemed to be *supernatural* creatures with a human torso, two heads (a human and a non-human one), and four legs.

This news worried Atahualpa. As Pizarro and his soldiers made their way inland, attacking villages along the way, Atahualpa's messengers told the Inca emperor about every detail of their progress.

*T*he Inca constructed their large stone temples and palaces without using cement or mortar. To lift the stones into place they used only ramps, logs, and levers. Many of these impressive structures are so strong that they still stand today, despite earthquakes that periodically strike the region. In May 1950, for example, an earthquake shook the Peruvian city of Cuzco and toppled many of the 400-year-old structures built by the Spanish explorers. But some buildings that were much older—and had been built by the Inca—survived. One writer described these buildings as having "finely crafted walls that the Incas had painstakingly fitted together without benefit of mortar, five centuries before."

For Francisco Pizarro, the way to escape the poverty he had been born into was to become a soldier. He was part of a Spanish army that fought in Italy, then he traveled to the New World in 1502.

Who Was Francisco Pizarro? 2

rancisco Pizarro, the man who was leading this strange expedition into the Inca empire, was born around the year 1471 in Trujillo, a town in the ***province*** known as Extremadura, in Spain.

Extremadura, near the present-day border of Portugal, was the poorest area of the country. Farming in the region was difficult, and few of the young men of Extremadura could make a living at it. Instead, many of them decided to seek their fortunes as soldiers. As a result, many of Spain's most famous ***conquistadors*** (or conquerors) came from Extremadura.

Francisco's father was a colonel in the Spanish army. Some historians report that his mother was a prostitute. Because Francisco's parents were not married, his birth was not listed in church records. Therefore, little is known about his early years. He was probably raised by his father's family. Later, several half-brothers would accompany him on his mission of conquest in the New World. Like most poor children in the region, Francisco did not attend school. Instead, he worked on a pig farm. It seemed that he would not amount to much, but Francisco longed for adventure and glory. When he was a teenager, he joined the Spanish army.

At that time, Spain was very different than it is today. It was broken into three countries: Castile and Aragon, where most of the people were Catholic; and Granada, which was controlled by the *Moors*. These were people from northern Africa who followed a religion called Islam. For the Catholic people of Castile and Aragon, the defeat of the Moors was very important. The two sides had been fighting for hundreds of years.

In 1492, when Pizarro was about 20 years old, the Spanish forces finally drove the Moors out of Granada. Afterwards, King Ferdinand of Aragon

This Arab tapestry shows Spaniards and Moors fighting in the city of Mallorca. Like many conquistadors, Pizarro gained battle experience in Spain's wars against the Moors and other enemies. This would prove useful in the New World.

and Queen Isabella of Castile ruled together over a newly united and fiercely Christian nation: Spain.

Spain was not the only European country that was changing. The world as Europeans knew it was rapidly expanding. Sailors from Portugal had been exploring to the south, seeking a sea route east to the Spice Islands and China, which were known as the East Indies. Products from the East Indies were valuable in Europe because they were very hard to get. A nation that could trade with the East Indies would quickly become very rich.

In 1492, the king and queen of Spain hired an Italian sailor named Christopher Columbus to sail into the unknown Atlantic Ocean. Columbus was

Christopher Columbus claims land in the New World. Columbus's 1492 voyage gave Spain an enormous new source of wealth. Brave men were needed to explore the new lands and find riches for their king.

trying to reach the East Indies by sailing west. When he spotted land after 33 days at sea, he believed he had found China. However, the islands he reached were actually in the Caribbean. Without realizing it, he had stumbled upon the "New World."

Soon it was clear that Columbus had actually found enormous lands that had been unknown to the Europeans of his time. The rulers of Spain were determined to be the first to explore and claim these vast unknown regions. Spain was a competitor with Portugal, and both countries struggled to be the first to *plunder* the riches of the new lands, expand their territories and trade routes, establish *colonies* overseas, and convert native peoples to Christianity.

The conquistadors who traveled to the New World wanted to claim land for the king and queen of Spain and to convert the native peoples to their own religion. But most of all, they sought gold and wealth. These goals, and a thirst for adventure, moved men to travel for months across dangerous seas in cramped, dirty ships, in the hope of reaching the New World. Throughout these expeditions, they faced disease and starvation, and along the way they prayed to be spared from storms and shipwreck.

Meanwhile, Francisco Pizarro worked hard for a

The Spanish felt that converting natives to Christianity was very important. They believed that Jesus Christ would return at the end of the world and that when he did, everyone should be Christian. They also believed that they could get into heaven by bringing this "true faith" to others who had never heard of Christ.

dozen years or more in the Spanish army, fighting in Italy and Navarre (a territory between France and Spain that both countries wanted to rule). But he could not seem to advance in rank or earn more money. He soon concluded that his destiny, or at least some adventure, lay in the New World. Like many conquistadors, Pizarro dreamed of growing rich and powerful there. In 1502, when he was about 30 years old, he journeyed to a new Spanish settlement that had been established on the island of Hispaniola (the site of present-day Haiti and the Dominican Republic).

On Hispaniola, Pizarro's skill as a soldier finally attracted attention. His ambition, courage, and military experience won him places in several important expeditions to Central America.

One trip was with Alonso de Ojeda on an expedition to present-day Colombia in 1509. Ojeda founded a small settlement there called San Sebastián. But soon the angry natives around the settlement pinned down the Spaniards in their tiny fort. During this *siege*, Ojeda left San Sebastián for Hispaniola, where he intended to gather reinforcements. He left Francisco Pizarro in charge, trusting him to hold onto the fort and the territory. Pizarro

Vasco Núñez de Balboa views the Pacific Ocean, the first time a European had seen the great body of water. Pizarro accompanied Balboa on this 1513 expedition.

was able to hold out for two months. Then he led the colonists and soldiers of San Sebastián back to the safety of Hispaniola.

After this adventure, Pizarro traveled with Vasco Núñez de Balboa on a journey to Panama. On the east coast of this land, Pizarro helped organize the Spanish settlement of Darién. In 1513, Balboa seized Darién from its commander. With some friendly natives and about 190 Spanish soldiers he traveled across the mountains of the **Isthmus** of Panama. On September 25 of that year, Balboa became the first European to see the Pacific coast of South America, which he claimed for Spain. The journals kept by members of the expedition claim that Pizarro was the second to see the Pacific (Balboa called it the South Sea). The group stayed there for a time and gathered gold and pearls before returning to Darién in January 1514.

Four years later, Pizarro was serving as a lieutenant to Governor Pedrarias of Panama when he was required to arrest his former friend and commander, Balboa. Balboa was charged with **treason** for seizing Darién, and he was executed in January 1519. Pizarro himself then became the mayor of Panama, where he served from 1519 to 1523. He was now in his fifties, yet his greatest achievements still lay ahead of him.

Rumors of a great and wealthy civilization to the south of Panama fed Pizarro's dreams of glory. He formed a partnership with a fellow soldier, Diego de Almagro, and a priest named Hernando de Luque. Luque agreed to provide money so that Pizarro and Almagro could explore. All three agreed to divide any treasure they gained during the expedition.

Pizarro and Almagro set to work gathering supplies and a force of men. Finally, in November 1524, Pizarro set sail southward from Panama. The crew traveled in two ships that carried about 140 soldiers, a few horses, and weapons such as guns, swords, crossbows, and lances. The ships also carried food supplies, including kegs of wine and drinking water, beans, bread, flour, and live chickens and pigs (which they would slaughter for meat). Almagro remained behind, planning to gather more men and supplies and meet up with Pizarro's forces later in the expedition.

Pizarro's soldiers knew that their journey would be dangerous. They may even have known that they would not all survive. But they felt certain that no matter what happened, the wonders of the New World awaited them. The vision of mountains of gold rising higher than any of the men could imagine kept their spirits high.

The Long
Quest Begins 3

he 1524 expedition was slowed by great storms and by contrary winds and currents. But the real danger to the Spaniards of Pizarro's expedition came upon their arrival in the unknown land. The crew encountered some natives along the Pacific coastline of northwest South America, but the people fled at the sight of the newcomers. While waiting for Almagro, however, the small army soon ran out of food. They had reached as far as the border between present-day Ecuador and Colombia.

Stuck in the jungle, with his men reduced to boiling belts and shoe leather for food, Pizarro managed to keep

The conquistador Diego de Almagro formed a partnership with Pizarro and a priest named Hernando de Luque. The three ambitious men saw a chance to get rich in the New World. The priest would provide funds, and the two soldiers would explore and conquer.

control of his miserable and frustrated soldiers. He sent half of the men toward the closest Spanish settlement to bring back food and supplies. Then Pizarro and the remaining 50 soldiers explored the surrounding area, surviving on shellfish gathered from the shoreline and wild berries and herbs they collected in the forest. Still, half of the men died in the six weeks before the supply party returned. Pizarro named this place Puerto de la Hambre, "Port of Hunger."

Undaunted by these misfortunes, Pizarro and his crew sailed farther south. They encountered a native town, but they were attacked there. Five Spanish soldiers died in the fighting and Pizarro himself was wounded seven times. While this was happening, Almagro had already begun his journey back, but he was having great difficulty finding Pizarro. He too faced conflict with the natives: he was wounded in an **ambush** and lost an eye.

Pizarro and Almagro finally did meet. Each had managed to accumulate some gold, and they were both sure that greater treasure could be found farther south. But the group was in no shape to continue. Instead, Pizarro and Almagro decided to return to Panama and raise a greater force for a fresh, new expedition.

In Panama, Pizarro, Almagro, and Luque drew up a formal contract in which they agreed to split all riches equally. After preparing for the journey, Almagro and Pizarro set sail again in 1526, this time with 10 ships. When they arrived at their destination, the commanders stole gold and ornaments from several village populations along the coast. Then they discovered a large city, Tacamez, where they were not welcome. A native army of perhaps 10,000 was ready to attack them.

Just then, however, a Spanish soldier's horse reared and threw its rider. The native people were stunned to see that this animal, which they thought was a single creature, had divided itself into two. They were so amazed that they did not attack, and the Spaniards were able to get back to their ships without being harmed. After this incident, the three partners agreed that they needed even more soldiers for their expedition. Almagro took the gold they had plundered back to Panama, where he planned to use the money to recruit more men.

But Almagro was in for a rude shock. In Panama a new royal governor, Pedro de los Rios, refused to support the expedition. Disgusted at the loss of Spanish lives during the voyage, Rios sent a messenger to Pizarro with a letter, urging Pizarro's men to return to Panama at once.

When the men heard this message, they cheered; they were miserable and wanted to go home. Pizarro took action. He boldly drew a line in the sand, declaring that each man had to choose whether to return to the safety of Panama or press on. Pointing to the line, he declared: "Friends and comrades, on that side [of the line] are toil, hunger, nakedness, the drenching storm, desertion, and death; on this side [are] ease and pleasure. There lies Peru and its riches; here [lies] Panama and poverty.

Choose, each man, what best becomes a brave Castilian [a resident of Castile, a region of Spain]. For my part, I go to the south."

Then Pizarro stepped over the line he had drawn. Only 13 others followed him. One of these, Bartolomé Ruiz, was the **navigator** of the expedition. Pizarro appointed him the task of taking back to Panama those who wished to abandon the expedition. They numbered nearly 200 men. Ruiz, Pizarro hoped, would then be able to return with more soldiers to replace those who had gone home.

Meanwhile, Pizarro's tiny Spanish force sailed to the south, crossing the equator. It landed at the town of Tumbes in what is now northwest Peru. Pizarro charmed the city's chief, who honored the strangers with food served on silver and gold platters. Pizarro hoped to win over the native people by restraining his greedy men, so at first he refused the gifts the natives offered the Spaniards. Eventually, though, the Spaniards sailed back to Panama not only with South American treasures but also with three inhabitants of Tumbes, including a man named Felipillo who served as an interpreter.

When Francisco Pizarro returned to Panama, he was bursting with the stories he had heard of a "city

In 1528, Francisco Pizarro left the New World for
Spain, where he asked King Charles V, pictured above,
to let him explore and conquer Peru.

to the south that blazed with gold and silver." He
was eager to return to Peru with reinforcements. But
the governor of Panama was unmoved by Pizarro's
tale of adventure and by the gold he brought back.
Pizarro and his partners refused to give in. If the

governor would not support their quest, they decided, then they would seek the approval of Charles V, the Spanish king himself. Pizarro, who was charming and confident, was chosen to approach the king. In 1528, he sailed to Spain.

Pizarro successfully gained a chance to meet with the mighty King Charles, and he showed the monarch evidence of his adventures in the New World: llama fleece, a newly drawn map of Peru, jewels, and gold. The simply dressed soldier also told the king that many natives could be baptized as Christians. And when Pizarro described how he and his small band of soldiers had survived for months in Peru, Charles V reportedly wept. A few months later, the king signed the document granting Pizarro permission to conquer Peru. Charles V declared Pizarro the governor of "New Castile" (Peru) and of all the settlements he established there. As a representative and subject of Charles V, Pizarro would be paid an annual salary. Charles himself would receive one-fifth of whatever goods and wealth Pizarro and his partners acquired.

In January 1530, Pizarro once again set sail for the New World. Diego de Almagro and Hernando de Luque eagerly awaited Pizarro's return to South

Before he returned to South America, Pizarro recruited several relatives from his hometown of Trujillo. His half-brothers Juan, Gonzalo, Martín, and Hernando eagerly joined Francisco's ambitious quest. Another relative, 15-year-old Pedro, was a servant. Years later, Pedro would write an account of Pizarro's conquest of the Inca empire.

America. But when they learned the details of his agreement with Charles V, they grew angry. The king had provided titles and responsibilities for the two men: Luque was declared bishop of Tumbes and "protector of the Indians," and Almagro was named the commander of Tumbes. But instead of being equal partners with Pizarro, they had received much less power. They would also get a smaller share in any riches they found. Pizarro insisted that the king had wanted one supreme commander, but he agreed to share the wealth equally with his partners, just as they had originally decided.

In 1531 Pizarro's force left Panama in three ships carrying 180 men and 27 horses; again, Almagro was scheduled to follow later. But Pizarro, now 60 years old, became frustrated by the slow pace of sailing the coast, and soon he decided to abandon the ships and travel by land. The Spaniards were wel-comed in the Coaque province, but they looted the Coaque villages of their gold and gems. Pizarro sent much of the wealth back to Panama, thinking that it would encourage more soldiers to join his army. Meanwhile, Pizarro's crew suffered from native attacks, diseases and infections, and blinding sand-storms. Several men died during these ordeals.

Just before the rainy winter season, a Spaniard named Hernando de Soto arrived with 100 men. Another 30 men arrived under the command of Sebastián de Belalcázar. During the winter the men reached Tumbes, but they found it destroyed. Pizarro then learned about the civil war that was dividing the Inca empire. He began the march southward, but he allowed those who wished to turn back to return to Panama. Only nine men did so; now the army numbered 168 men. With this small force, Pizarro headed for Cajamarca. He had learned that Atahualpa was camped there.

The Conquest
of Peru

As the outnumbered Spaniards fought the Inca, Pizarro and his men forced their way through the crowd to Atahualpa. When Pizarro seized the Inca ruler, the native warriors gave up the fight and fled. Many were slaughtered by the Spaniards.

4

rancisco Pizarro was in a great hurry to reach Cajamarca, so he decided to cross the Andes Mountains rather than go around them. Glaciers and ice towered above the men, who forced their frightened horses along narrow rock ledges atop cliffs dropping hundreds of feet. At every turn they feared an Inca force would ambush them. At last, the Spaniards descended into a river valley and gazed upon the beautiful city of Cajamarca.

The city was empty.

As the Spaniards had neared Cajamarca, Atahualpa had begun sending messages. At first the messages welcomed the strangers, but then they began warning Pizarro not to enter the city. Pizarro had no intention of turning back—especially after seeing the gold worn by the Inca messengers. Because the Spaniards continued to approach even after they had been warned, Atahualpa had ordered his people to abandon Cajamarca.

Atahualpa's enormous army waited three miles outside the city. But it did not attack, even though the Inca greatly outnumbered the Spaniards.

Pizarro and his army marched into Cajamarca and occupied the city. Then Pizarro sent a message to Atahualpa requesting that the Sapa Inca join him and

Even though an Inca army of 40,000 waited outside the city, Pizarro decided to occupy Cajamarca. "It was unwise to show any fear," he later wrote. "We had to go into the town. So with a show of good spirits, we descended into the valley. . . . The most sensible course was to make as bold an appearance as possible and continue openly without any apparent fear or regard for the Incas."

his men for a special banquet the following day. Twenty mounted and armored Spanish soldiers, led by Hernando Pizarro and Hernando de Soto, carried the message.

While Hernando Pizarro and de Soto were meeting with Atahualpa, de Soto noticed the Sapa Inca's curious glances at his horse. The Spaniard impulsively mounted the animal and took it on a flashy and impressive ride. De Soto charged at the Sapa Inca himself, but he halted his horse just shy of the emperor. Atahualpa did not flinch, but others around him did. Later that evening, the Inca chief ordered those who had done so to be executed for showing fear before the strangers.

Atahualpa agreed to meet Francisco Pizarro in Cajamarca the next day. Pizarro was delighted. He remembered the cunning charm that another conquistador, Hernando Cortés, had used to capture the great Aztec emperor Montezuma years before in Mexico. Pizarro decided that he would try to trick Atahualpa in the same way that Cortés had deceived Montezuma.

The Spaniards waited all day for Atahualpa to appear. Finally, as the sun was setting, the Inca emperor arrived in Cajamarca. He was carried on a *litter*, or platform, by 80 men. Behind them were several hundred of his best warriors.

The only strangers who greeted him were Felip-illo, the native interpreter, and a friar named Vicente de Valverde. The friar gave Atahualpa a Bible and explained to the Inca chief that he must convert to Christianity and swear allegiance to Charles V of Spain.

Atahualpa was angry. He had heard reports about these Spaniards looting his villages. Also, he did not feel that he should give up his religion for that of the newcomers. "Your own God, as you say, was put to death by the very men he created," Atahualpa said to Valverde, referring to Jesus. "But mine," he continued, pointing to the sun, "still lives and looks down on his children." Then Atahualpa tossed the Bible to the ground.

At that moment, Pizarro, who was hidden in a nearby building watching the confrontation, gave a signal. Suddenly, a Spanish cannon began to fire, and soldiers sprang up from what seemed like thin air. They attacked the Inca.

Then Hernando de Soto and Hernando Pizarro, shouting battle cries, led their mounted troops into the fray. At the same time, Francisco Pizarro led his

Spanish friar Vicente de Valverde preaches Christianity to Atahualpa. When the Inca ruler rejected the priest's message, the Spaniards attacked.

20 soldiers across the square, fighting through Atahualpa's guard until they grasped the Inca ruler.

Seeing their leader captured, the demoralized

When Atahualpa was captured, Inca resistance melted away. Fearing for his life, the ruler promised to give the Spaniards a room full of gold if they would spare him.

Indians broke and ran from the battlefield. The Spaniards chased the fleeing Inca warriors. The bloody massacre left more than 2,000 Inca soldiers dead. Not a single Spaniard was killed; the only wound was received by Pizarro himself, who was badly cut as he captured Atahualpa. The powerful Inca ruler, worshiped as a god by millions of people, was now the prisoner of Pizarro.

After the massacre in the square of Cajamarca, the Spaniards looted the city, uncovering huge stores of gold and silver platters and other objects in the Sapa Inca's palace. The captured leader was permitted to live as he had before the attack, in his palace surrounded by his royal servants and his wives. But Atahualpa worried that now his brother Huáscar would escape and declare himself the new Sapa Inca. He needed to be free to fight for his empire.

Atahualpa quickly discovered that gold and other riches were the way to win over the white men. He offered Pizarro and his men a large ransom—a room full of gold and two rooms full of silver—in exchange for his freedom. Not content with the riches he had found so far, Pizarro agreed to release Atahualpa.

Atahualpa sent for the gold, which soon began arriving from across the Inca empire. Scores of delicately crafted ornaments and other objects were melted down, formed into bars, and stamped with the seal of Charles V for shipment to Spain.

Still, Pizarro was suspicious of the Sapa Inca. He continually sent bands of soldiers to various cities throughout the empire to make certain that no rebellion was being planned in Atahualpa's name. Meanwhile, Pizarro's half-brother Hernando and Hernando de Soto became friends with Atahualpa.

While the Inca gold was being collected and sent to Cajamarca to be given to Pizarro, Atahualpa learned that his brother Huáscar had offered even more gold to the Spaniards if they would free him and restore his title. Francisco Pizarro had his own worries: Almagro arrived with 150 men and demanded his share of the riches (Luque had died in Panama).

> The Spaniards eventually collected 24 tons of gold as ransom for Atahualpa. Today that would be worth $1.6 billion!

Almagro and Hernando Pizarro greatly disliked each other, and Almagro was suspicious of Hernando's friendship with the Inca emperor. Francisco Pizarro decided to send his half-brother back to Spain with Charles V's share of the wealth. In 1533, the year after Pizarro and his men arrived in Cajamarca, the treasure was divided among the Spaniards, with a smaller share going to Almagro's men. This crew expected to make up the difference by conquering the capital city of Cuzco.

Like Hernando Pizarro, Hernando de Soto was also sent away. Pizarro ordered de Soto to visit far-away areas of the Inca empire, to insure that no attack against Cajamarca was being planned.

Once these two influential leaders were out of the way, Francisco Pizarro and Almagro staged a trial for Atahualpa. But instead of freeing the chief as he had promised, Pizarro sentenced Atahualpa to death by burning. As was the custom in Spain, Friar Valverde offered Atahualpa an easier death if he would agree to be baptized a Christian. That night, Atahualpa was given the name Juan de Atahualpa, and, as he gazed steadily at Pizarro, the Inca emperor was strangled.

Hernando de Soto was a key member of Pizarro's expedition to Peru. De Soto later attempted an expedition of his own. From 1539 to 1542 de Soto and his men explored Florida and much of the American South. They did not find gold, and de Soto died on the journey.

Having conquered the wealthiest empire in South America, Pizarro now took complete control of the region. The Inca had lost their god and emperor, so they began burying gold and treasure to keep it from the Spaniards. Pizarro's men ruthlessly looted and plundered. They even stole from Inca temples and graves. All across the empire, some continued to resist the white-skinned invaders, staging ambushes and attacks whenever they had the chance. But Pizarro responded with brutality, killing thousands in *retaliation* for their assaults.

Finally, Pizarro decided that he needed to do something to quell the Inca uprisings. He announced that he wanted Huáscar's younger brother to rule the Inca. Pizarro hoped that when he had restored the title of Sapa Inca, the native population would cease its attacks. In 1535 Pizarro crowned Huáscar's younger brother Manco Capac II, emperor of the Inca in Cuzco.

All those who helped conquer the Inca became exceptionally rich. Even the lowest-ranking soldiers received a share of the plunder. Francisco Pizarro received enough from the capture of Cajamarca alone to make him one of the richest men in Spain

Still hungry for glory, Pizarro aimed to make his colony in South America even more prosperous than the Spanish colony in Panama. To do this, he set about building a new capital city to replace Cuzco. The new capital, called Lima, was situated on the coast of what is now Peru. Lima remains the capital of Peru today.

While Pizarro was claiming his territory and building his reputation, Almagro led his men to what is now Chile. There, he hoped to plunder still more gold and silver.

A Bloody End

Pizarro's conquest of the Inca made him one of the richest men in Spain, but he would not live long enough to enjoy his money. Pizarro was murdered by political enemies in 1541. Yet he is remembered both in Spain and in South America. This statue of Pizarro stands outside the Church of San Martín in Trujillo, Peru.

5

The new Sapa Inca, Manco Capac II, was not about to let the Spaniard Pizarro take over his empire. In 1536, while Pizarro was founding Lima and Almagro was headed toward Chile, Manco staged an attack against the Spaniards whom Pizarro had left to guard the city. The Inca soldiers shot flaming arrows into the thatched roofs of Cuzco and ignited them. Almost the entire city burned. With the remaining conquistadors in total disarray, Manco

> **One of the Spaniards killed during the Inca uprising in Cuzco was Francisco Pizarro's brother Juan.**

and his men attacked. After a fierce struggle, however, the Spanish defenders' cannons and their cavalry, which was led by Hernando Pizarro, forced the Inca attackers to retreat. When the native warriors broke away and ran, they were pursued and hacked to death. The major battle had ended, but random attacks continued in and around Cuzco.

Meanwhile, in Lima, Francisco Pizarro was also besieged by Inca warriors. He finally managed to drive away the attackers. But the city of Cuzco fell the following spring–not to Manco, but to Diego de Almagro's returning army, which captured the city. Almagro did not trust Hernando Pizarro, who had commanded the Spanish forces in Cuzco, so he took Francisco's brother prisoner.

Francisco Pizarro agreed to Almagro's demand that he be named commander of Cuzco. However, Pizarro would not let him take over until Charles V officially decided who would rule the city. In exchange, Almagro promised to free Hernando Pizarro. Almagro was as good as his word–but he should not have trusted Francisco. Once Hernando was freed, the Pizarro brothers united their armies and warned Almagro to prepare to battle for control of Cuzco.

In April 1538, Hernando Pizarro's men attacked Diego de Almagro's forces near Cuzco. The Incas looked on with satisfaction as the two groups of Spaniards fought each other in the battle that became known as Las Salinas. Hernando Pizarro won the battle, which claimed 150 lives. He took the aging Almagro prisoner, and then watched as his former comrade was executed.

Francisco Pizarro applauded his brother's action. He took control of Almagro's share of the former Inca empire. In doing so, he **alienated** Almagro's son by stripping him of his father's possessions. Then he sought to defeat Manco once and for all by publicly torturing and killing the Sapa Inca's wife. Such cruelty only angered the Inca further, and they grew even more determined to fight the invading Spaniards as long as they could.

Tales about Pizarro's conquest of the Inca empire spread, and they made Pizarro a legend in Spain as well as among other Spaniards exploring the New World. Furthermore, King Charles was

Although he was a successful conqueror and explorer, Francisco Pizarro was not a very honorable man. He broke his word whenever it was to his advantage to do so, as in the execution of Atahualpa and in the fight against Almagro.

extremely grateful to Pizarro—and rightfully so. The conquistador had expanded Charles's kingdom into a new continent and added untold amounts of gold to the royal treasury. Still, Charles was angered by Francisco and Hernando Pizarro's actions against Diego de Almagro. He was also upset about the continuing chaos in Peru. The king ordered Hernando Pizarro to return to Spain and account for his conduct. There, Hernando languished in prison from 1539 to 1561.

Francisco Pizarro's contributions to the history of South America were not yet finished, however. He sent a soldier named Pedro de Valdivia to explore Chile. Pizarro sent another expedition, led by his half-brother Gonzalo Pizarro, to northern South America. While searching for a mythical land of gold called El Dorado, Gonzalo and Francisco de Orellana discovered the mouth of the Napo River, in present-day Ecuador.

Orellana was ordered to follow the river downstream and return with supplies and food. He sailed down the river as ordered, but the current was more powerful than he had expected. He soon realized that he could not possibly return the same way he had come. When the Napo River emptied into a larger waterway, he decided to follow the bigger river to its mouth. Thus he became the first European to navigate the largest river in the world—the Amazon—from its source to its mouth. The small party was lucky to have survived the raging waters.

Francisco Pizarro was now in his seventies, but he still ruled his territory with an iron fist. What's more, the hostility between Pizarro and Almagro's supporters had never gone away, and there were many rumors of plots against Pizarro's life. He learned about one of these plots on June 26, 1541, but he did not pay much attention to the rumor.

That day, however, Pizarro was having lunch with his captains and some officials when several Almagro supporters broke into his palace at Lima. Pizarro fought back, but there were too many attackers, and they were brutal. One account by a writer of the time says that during the onslaught Pizarro "called out the name of Jesus. With blood from his own wounds he drew a Christian cross on the floor and reached out to kiss it. But before he could do so, a final blow put an end to his extraordinary career."

During his lifetime, Pizarro transformed the history of Peru. He and other Spanish conquistadors had placed the great wealth of all of Peru in the hands of just a few Europeans.

After the Spanish had arrived in South America and conquered the Inca, they had enforced a system called *encomienda*. In this system, the Spaniards forced the Inca to pay *tribute* to them by working their own lands. In return, the Spanish protected the natives. But encomienda, which was put into practice wherever the Spaniards settled in the New World, practically enslaved native peoples. Most of their gold and silver was melted down and sent to Spain; Spain would then squander the treasure on European wars.

The natives of Peru consider Atahualpa, rather than Pizarro, to be the true hero of the conquest. This portrait of Atahualpa was part of a collection of paintings of Inca chiefs commissioned by the Spaniards after the conquest of Peru.

Because of the brutal treatment of native South Americans by the Spanish conquistadors, there remains much resentment toward Francisco Pizarro. For many Peruvians, the great hero of the conquest of 1532 is not Pizarro but Atahualpa, the last reigning Inca emperor. Later leaders, like Manco Capac II and Sayri Tupac, struggled to resist the Spaniards and maintain control of a small area in the former Inca empire, which was called Vilcabamba. But in 1572, even this last outpost collapsed.

Shortly after the conquest, Catholic missionaries arrived to convert and instruct the natives in the

Pizarro and other conquistadors brought Spanish religion
and culture to the natives of the Americas. This native
painting on cloth shows Indians being baptized.

Christian faith. Other Spaniards began marrying
Indians. Their children, people of mixed Spanish
and Native American ancestry, were called *mestizos*.

Today, mestizos make up the majority of the people in the lands the Spanish conquered. But native
languages like Quechua and Aymara are still spoken
by millions of people in Peru, and other aspects of
Inca life remain remarkably constant. For example,

women in the Peruvian highlands still weave cloth and wear garments similar to those of the Inca. Corn and potatoes are still grown, and llamas and alpacas are still raised to provide wool. In rural communities in particular, neighbors are quick to help one another, just as they were required to do under Inca rule. Even Catholic festivals such as Corpus Christi, and the important pilgrimage to Qoyllur Rit'i, retain elements of the ancient Inca religion.

The influence of Pizarro and other early Spanish adventurers on the area is still apparent as well. Most of the people living in Peru are Catholic, for example, and Spanish is the official national language. Many of the country's traditional dishes are a mixture of Spanish and Native American styles of food, and its art, music, and culture retain strong Spanish influences.

By today's standards, Francisco Pizarro and other conquistadors were certainly ruthless, cruel men at times. Whatever modern South Americans feel about the controversial Francisco Pizarro, he was undoubtedly a good general and a courageous explorer.

Chronology

1200 Inca civilization begins with the founding of Cuzco in present-day Peru.

1471 Francisco Pizarro is born near Trujillo, in Extremadura, Spain.

1492 Christopher Columbus arrives in Hispaniola; the Inca people conquer what is now Chile.

1500 Pedro Cabral claims Brazil for Portugal; the mouth of the Amazon River is discovered by Europeans; Amerigo Vespucci begins exploring the coast of South America.

1502 Columbus reaches Panama on his fourth voyage; Francisco Pizarro sails to Hispaniola.

1509 Pizarro accompanies Alonso de Ojeda to Colombia in
–10 1509 and accompanies Vasco Núñez de Balboa to Panama the next year.

1513 Spanish explorers reach the Pacific Ocean in Panama.

1519 Pizarro is named mayor of Panama and serves until 1523.

1524 Francisco Pizarro and Diego de Almagro lead an
–26 expedition to Ecuador and Colombia; they return to Panama in 1525 and sail for Peru in 1526.

1527 Pizarro discovers the Inca empire; after the Spaniards depart, 200,000 Inca people, including Sapa Inca Huayna Capac, succumb to an epidemic.

1528 Civil war rages between Huáscar and his brother
–32 Atahualpa; Atahualpa defeats Huáscar; in 1528 Pizarro returns to Spain to gather support for an expedition against the Inca empire.

1530 Pizarro leaves Spain after recruiting half-brothers Juan,
 −31 Martín, Hernando, and Gonzalo; he embarks on his third
      expedition to Peru.

1532 Pizarro attacks the Incas at Cajamarca and takes Atahualpa
 −33 prisoner; despite a huge ransom in gold, Atahualpa is exe-
      cuted and the Spaniards capture Cuzco four months later.

1535 Pizarro founds the city of Lima and names Manco Capac
 −36 as Inca ruler; in 1536 Manco Capac attacks the Spaniards
      at Cuzco but fails; disputes arise between Pizarro and
      Almagro.

1538 Pizarro executes Almagro.

1540 Gonzalo Pizarro and Francisco de Orellana begin their
 −41 expedition to find El Dorado.

1541 Pizarro is assassinated on June 26.

1572 Topa Amaru, the last Inca ruler, is executed when Spain
      captures Vilcabamba.

1580 Six million Inca have died since the Spanish arrival in
      South America.

1911 The ancient Inca ruins of Machu Picchu are discovered by
      Hiram Bingham.

Glossary

adobe–a brick or other object made of sun-dried earth and straw, or a building made from such materials.

alienate–to cause to become unfriendly or hostile.

alpacas–mammals with fine, long, wooly hair that are native to Peru.

ambush–a trap set by lying in wait and then attacking by surprise.

benevolent–marked by doing good or having goodwill.

civil war–a war between opposing groups of citizens of the same country.

colony–a group of people living in a new territory but keeping ties with a parent state.

conquistadors–Spanish soldiers who conquered native tribes.

descendant–a direct relative of a person from an earlier generation. (For example, you are the descendant of your parents and grandparents.)

encomienda–a system established by Spanish explorers that required conquered natives to pay tribute in the form of labor. In return, the natives would receive protection from the Spaniards. In practice, the harsh system was much like slavery.

immunity–a quality or state in which the body is able to resist a harmful disease.

irrigation–a system in which an area of land is supplied with water by artificial means such as pipes or canals.

isthmus–a narrow strip of land connecting two larger land areas.

litter–a platform used to carry a single person.

mestizos–people of mixed Native American and Spanish ancestry.

Moors–a group of people from North Africa that invaded Spain in the eighth century. The Moors were involved in a series of bloody wars with the Christian people of Spain. The Moors were forced out of Spain in 1492.

navigator–a person who sets the course for a journey or who steers the vehicle used for the journey.

plunder–to take by force or by theft.

populated–filled with people.

province–a region of a country, usually separated from other provinces by geographical or political boundaries.

Quechua–the native language of the Inca.

relief map–a type of map showing the elevation (height) of the land.

retaliation–a repayment in kind; revenge.

siege–a prolonged attack or a blocking of a fortified place that is meant to force its inhabitants to surrender.

smelt–to melt metals to separate or fuse them and create new materials.

supernatural–existing beyond the visible or observable world.

treason–an offense of attempting to overthrow a government or ruler to which the offender owes loyalty.

tribute–payment by one ruler or nation to another in exchange for protection or as a sign of submission.

Further Reading

Bernhard, Brendan. *Pizarro, Orellana, and the Exploration of the Amazon.* New York: Chelsea House Publishers, 1991.

Chrisp, Peter. *The Spanish Conquests in the New World.* New York: Thomson Learning, 1993.

De Angelis, Therese. *Native Americans and the Spanish.* Philadelphia: Chelsea House, 1997.

Faber, Harold. *The Discoverers of America.* New York: Charles Scribner's Sons, 1992.

Gaffron, Norma. *El Dorado, Land of Gold.* San Diego: Greenhaven Press, 1990.

Hinds, Kathryn. *The Incas.* New York: Benchmark Books, 1998.

Jacobs, William Jay. *Pizarro: Conqueror of Peru.* New York and Chicago: Franklin Watts, 1994.

Lourie, Peter. *Lost Treasure of the Incas.* Honesdale, Pa.: Boyds Mills Press, 1999.

Marrin, Albert. *Inca and Spaniard: Pizarro and the Conquest of Peru.* New York: Atheneum, 1989.

Rees, Rosemary. *The Incas.* Des Plaines, Ill.: Heinemann Library, 1999.

Sayer, Chloë. *The Incas.* Austin, Tex.: Steck-Vaughn, 1999.

Steele, Philip. *The Incas and Machu Picchu.* New York: Dillon Press, 1993.

Wood, Tim. *The Incas.* New York: Viking, 1996.

Picture Credits

GINA DEANGELIS earned her B.A. in theater and history and her M.A. in history. She is the author of several young adult books in biography, history, and other subjects, and has written plays and screenplays as well. She lives in Virginia with her daughter and pet gerbils.